GIRLS & BOYS

EASY-TO-COOK BOOK

Recipes by ANN WAINWRIGHT

Edited by BARBARA ZEITZ

Illustrated by STAN TUSAN

Introduction by POPPY CANNON

GROSSET & DUNLAP · NEW YORK

By special arrangement with Wonder Books

Introduction

Children beware! Mommas, poppas and older sisters cannot be trusted. When they leaf through GIRLS AND BOYS EASY-TO-COOK-BOOK, they are tempted to make off with it ... First they say "it's just to look at"... then "just to try." But how does a girl or boy make sure to get it back?

Stan Tusan has illustrated the merriest cookbook of the season — very clear, very usable — designed for beginners aged 7 and over. Recipes range from breakfasts, sandwiches and lunch, through burgers, snacks, dinner dishes, desserts, parties and special occasions.

Names are endearing, and there are many original touches. A combination of tomato soup and cheese is called The Red Robin. Midget Meat Loaves are baked in muffin tins — only 15 minutes. Tutti Fruity Pork Chops are cooked with pineapple chunks and orange juice. Tommy Tangburger is an open faced joy with the meat cooked right onto the bread. Peanut butter gets a great play. A Leprechaun Pie hobnobs with Porcupines, Pink Elephants, Shaggy Dogs and Chocolate Marshmallow Smudges. For Thanksgiving, there's a Name-Tag Pie, for Halloween, a Witches' Brew, for Happy Father's Day ... alphabet cereal coated with chocolate to spell out loving messages to Dad atop a cake.

Don't rob the young. Better buy two!

Poppy Cannon

Library of Congress Catalog Card No.: 67-19985

TABLE OF CONTENTS

Breakfast

SCRAMBLED EGGS
Serves 2 or 3

4 Eggs   *4 Tablespoons Milk*
Salt & Pepper (dash)   *1 Tablespoon Butter*

1. Break eggs into a small mixing bowl and beat with a fork.
2. Add salt, pepper and milk, and stir.
3. Heat butter in frying pan until bubbling and pour in egg mixture.
4. Cook slowly over low flame, stirring, until eggs hold together.

SCRAMBLED EGGS WITH CHEESE
Serves 2 or 3

Scrambled Eggs (this page)
½ cup American Cheese (grated)

1. Cook Scrambled Eggs until the eggs are soupy (not yet solid).
2. Add cheese and cook one more minute until the mixture holds together.

SCRAMBLED EGGS WITH BACON

Serves 2 or 3

Scrambled Eggs (page 5)
6 or 8 Slices Bacon

1. Place 6 or 8 slices of bacon in a cold frying pan and fry over medium heat.
2. When bacon is crisp on one side, turn and fry the other side. Drain on paper towels and keep in a warm oven.
3. Cook eggs as in Scrambled Eggs recipe (page 5).
4. Arrange bacon slices around the edges of a platter of eggs.

SCRAMBLED EGGS IN TOAST CUPS

Serves 2 or 3

Scrambled Eggs (page 5)   *Butter*
4 Slices White Bread

1. Cook Scrambled Eggs and keep them warm in a covered pan.
2. Remove crusts from bread. Butter a muffin tin and press bread into the cups.
3. Toast under the broiler until nicely browned.
4. Remove toast cups and fill with Scrambled Eggs.

SCRAMBLED EGGS WESTERN STYLE
Serves 2 or 3

Scrambled Eggs (page 5)
2 Tablespoons Butter
2 Tablespoons Minced Onion
2 Tablespoons Minced Green Pepper
4 Tablespoons Minced Cooked Ham

1. Melt butter in a small frying pan and cook the onions and green pepper until soft.
2. Cook the Scrambled Eggs until they are soupy (not yet solid).
3. Add the onion, green pepper and ham.
4. Cook a little longer until the mixture holds together.

TOAST

Toast can be a main course at breakfast, or you can serve it with any of the Scrambled Egg recipes. When the bread is nicely toasted, butter it and wrap in a napkin to keep it hot. Serve your favorite jam or jelly at the table. Toast can be made ahead of time and kept warm in the oven until the rest of your breakfast is ready.

CINNAMON TOAST
Serves 2 or 3

4 Slices Hot Buttered Toast　　*2 Tablespoons*
1 teaspoon Cinnamon　　　　　*Sugar*

1. Mix the cinnamon and sugar in a small dish.
2. Sprinkle over the toast and serve while it is still warm.

BANANA TOAST
Serves 2 or 3

4 Slices Hot Buttered Toast　　*2 Tablespoons*
2 Bananas　　　　　　　　　　*Brown Sugar*

1. Peel and slice the bananas.
2. Arrange the slices on the toast and sprinkle with brown sugar.
3. Put the toast on a cookie sheet and broil for a minute or two until the sugar is bubbly.

Let the Banana Toast cool slightly so you don't burn your tongue!

FRENCH TOAST
Serves 2 or 3

2 Eggs

½ teaspoon Salt

⅛ teaspoon Nutmeg

4 Tablespoons Sugar

¾ cup Cold Milk

1 Tablespoon Butter

6 to 8 Slices White Bread

1. With a fork lightly beat the eggs, salt, nutmeg, sugar and milk until well mixed.

2. Melt butter in frying pan and heat until butter begins to brown.

3. Dip each slice of bread in the egg batter until well soaked, and place in the frying pan to cook.

4. Cook one side until lightly browned and flip over to brown the other side.

You can keep the cooked French Toast hot in a warm oven until you've cooked all your bread. Serve hot with butter and syrup.

SUPER QUICK WAFFLE TREAT
Serves 2 or 3

3 Frozen Waffles (double)
1 Pint Vanilla Ice Cream   *Syrup*

1. Toast the waffles until they are browned and warm.
2. Add a scoop of ice cream and top with syrup.

This is a treat for a special occasion!

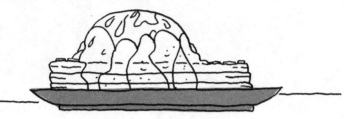

WAFFLES WITH ORANGE SAUCE
Serves 2 or 3

½ cup Sugar
½ cup Frozen Orange Juice Concentrate (thawed)
Salt, dash

2 Egg Yolks
1 cup Heavy Cream, whipped
1 Package Frozen Waffles (toasted)

1. In a saucepan, slowly cook the sugar, orange juice and salt until sugar is dissolved.
2. In a mixing bowl, beat the egg yolks lightly and pour in some of the orange mixture, beating as you pour.
3. Now pour this mixture into the saucepan and cook slowly until sauce is slightly thick.
4. Cool to room temperature and stir in the whipped cream. Refrigerate for about 1 hour before serving on waffles.

PANCAKES
Serves 2 or 3

1¼ cups Sifted Flour

2½ teaspoons Baking Powder

2 Tablespoons Sugar

¾ teaspoon Salt

1 Egg

1¼ cups Cold Milk

3 Tablespoons Butter (melted)

1. There are only two simple mixtures that go into homemade pancakes.
    — Sift together flour, baking powder, salt and sugar.
    — Lightly beat the egg, then add milk and melted butter.
2. Slowly pour the liquid into the flour mixture and stir just until mixed. Batter will be a little lumpy.
3. Heat your frying pan until hot but not smoking, and spoon out 1 Tablespoonful of batter for each pancake.
4. When bubbles appear in pancakes turn them over to brown the other side.

You can keep the pancakes hot in a warm oven until you've cooked enough for everyone. Serve with butter and syrup.

PANCAKES WITH RASPBERRY SAUCE
Serves 2 or 3

Pancakes (page 11)   *2 Tablespoons Butter*

½ cup Frozen Rasp-   *1 cup Pancake Syrup*
berries (thawed)

1. Cook the Pancakes and keep them hot in the oven.
2. In a saucepan slowly warm the raspberries, butter and syrup.
3. Pour into a sauce dish and serve with the hot Pancakes.

PINEAPPLE PANCAKES
Serves 2 or 3

½ cup Crushed Pineapple, drained (Save juice for Pineapple Syrup, page 13)

Pancakes (page 11)

1. Make the Pancake batter.
2. Stir in the pineapple and cook the Pancakes.

All you need is butter and syrup!

PINEAPPLE SYRUP
Serves 2 or 3

Pineapple Juice (saved from Pineapple Pancakes)
1 cup Syrup
2 Tablespoons Butter

1. In a saucepan slowly warm the pineapple juice, syrup and butter.
2. Pour into a sauce dish and serve with hot Pineapple Pancakes.

APPLE PANCAKES
Serves 2 or 3

Pancake Batter (page 11)
1 cup Apple, grated
1 Tablespoon Lemon Juice
2 Tablespoons Sugar

1. Make the Pancake batter.
2. Stir in the apple, lemon juice and sugar, and cook the Pancakes.

BLUEBERRY PANCAKES
Serves 2 or 3

Pancake Batter (page 11)
½ Pint Box Blueberries

1. Make the Pancake batter.
2. Spoon into frying pan to cook the pancakes and when bubbles appear sprinkle about 8 blueberries on each.
3. Flip the pancakes over to cook the other side.

Scrumptious, with butter and syrup!

BROILED GRAPEFRUIT

½ Grapefruit for each serving　　*Brown*
Maraschino Cherries　　　　　　　*Sugar*

1. Wash the grapefruit and cut in half crosswise. Loosen grapefruit sections around outer edge and between segments with a grapefruit knife. (Ask Mother to help you with this step.)
2. Place a cherry in the middle and sprinkle with brown sugar.
3. Broil for a few minutes until the sugar melts and is bubbly.

SUNDAY MORNING BREAKFAST SALAD
Serves 3 or 4

2 Oranges　　　　　*Small Bunch Grapes*
2 Bananas　　　　　*¼ cup Shredded Coconut*

1. Prepare the fruit: Peel the oranges and bananas and cut into bite size pieces. Slice grapes in half. (Be sure to remove any seeds.)
2. Toss the fruit together and refrigerate until very cold.
3. At the last minute add the coconut and toss lightly, mixing fruit and coconut.

Sandwiches & Lunch

HOT DOG SPECIAL
Serves 4

4 Hot Dogs

4 Slices Bacon

4 Slices American Cheese

8 Toothpicks (wooden)

1. Prepare your hot dogs and cheese: Slit the hot dogs lengthwise, but do not slice through. Cut all four cheese slices at once into 4 wedges.

2. Stuff the cheese wedges into the hot dogs and wrap a slice of bacon around to hold the cheese in.

3. Fasten the ends of the bacon with toothpicks and bake in a 400 degree oven until bacon is crisp.

BANANA BOATS
Serves 4

4 Hot Dog Rolls

2 Bananas, sliced

8 Slices Bacon

Peanut Butter

1. Peel and slice the bananas.

2. Fry the bacon until crisp.

3. Spread peanut butter on insides of rolls.

4. Arrange banana slices on one half, bacon strips on the other and close 'em up!

OPEN-FACE HAMBURGERS
Serves 2 or 3

¾ pound Ground Beef *Pepper, dash*
½ teaspoon salt *⅓ cup Evaporated Milk*
1½ Tablespoons Onion, *2 Hamburger Buns*
minced *(split)*

1. In a mixing bowl combine the meat, salt, pepper, onion and milk. Mix lightly with a fork.
2. Open the buns and toast the insides under the broiler.
3. Spread the hamburger mixture on the toasted buns (be sure to spread it out to the edges).
4. Broil for about 7 minutes, or until the hamburger is done.

OPEN-FACE CHEESEBURGERS
Serves 2 or 3

Open-Face Hamburgers (this page)
4 Slices American Cheese

1. Cook the Open-Face Hamburgers.
2. Place a slice of cheese on each and return to the broiler to melt and brown the cheese.

TOMMY TANGBURGERS

Serves 2 or 3

Open-Face Hamburgers
(page 16)
2 English Muffins
(split)

4 Slices Tomato
4 Slices Bacon
4 Slices American
Cheese

1. Make the Open-Face Hamburger mixture.
2. Toast the insides of the English Muffins.
3. Spread the hamburger mixture on the toasted muffins and top with cheese slices, tomato slices and bacon.
4. Broil for about 7 minutes until cheese is melted and bacon is crisp.

OPEN CHEESE SANDWICHES

Serves 2 or 3

2 Hamburger Buns,
(split) or,
4 Slices White Bread

8 Slices American
Cheese
Butter

1. Butter the bun halves (or bread) and put two slices of cheese on each.
2. Broil until the cheese melts and is lightly browned.

Serve with ripe olives, pickles or other relishes.

17

OPEN CHEESE FANCY
Serves 2 or 3

Open Cheese Sandwiches (page 17)
4 Tomato Slices
4 Slices Bacon, cut in half

1. Make Open Cheese Sandwiches.
2. Add a slice of tomato to each and crisscross bacon slices.
3. Broil until cheese is melted and bacon is crisp.

PEANUT BUTTER and . . .
PEANUT PARTY RIBBONS
Serves 2

4 Slices Bread (2 white, 1 rye, 1 whole wheat)

Peanut Butter

1. Starting with white bread, spread peanut butter on bread slices, one on top of the other, ending with white bread.
2. Trim crusts off, making the sides even.
3. Slice down (like thin-sliced cake) and there you have the party ribbons!

Arrange prettily on a plate and serve with lunch or after school for friends.

PEANUT BUTTER and . . .
CRISP BACON AND ·APPLES
Serves 2

½ cup Peanut Butter ¼ cup Apple, grated
3 Slices Bacon 4 Slices Bread

1. Prepare the bacon and apple: Fry bacon until crisp and, when it is cool, crumble between your fingers. Wash, peel and core the apple and then grate it.
2. Mix everything except the bread together in a small mixing bowl.
3. Spread on bread and cut in halves or fourths.

PEANUT BUTTER and . . .
NUTTY HONEY
Serves 2

½ cup Peanut Butter 2 Tablespoons Honey
2 Tablespoons Chopped 4 Slices Bread
Nuts

1. Mix everything except the bread together in a small mixing bowl.
2. Spread on bread and cut in halves or fourths.

PEANUT BUTTER and . . . BANANAS
Serves 2

½ cup Peanut Butter   Mayonnaise
1 Banana   4 Slices Bread

1. Peel and mash the banana with a fork.
2. Mix in the peanut butter and a little mayonnaise to make the mixture easy to spread.
3. Spread on bread and cut into halves or fourths.

PEANUT BUTTER and . . . HAM
Serves 2

1 Small Can Deviled   2 Tablespoons
  Ham   Mayonnaise
¼ cup Peanut Butter   2 teaspoons Mustard
    4 Slices Raisin Bread

1. Mix everything except bread together in a small mixing bowl.
2. Spread on the raisin bread and cut in halves or fourths.

20

PICKLE DOGS
Serves 4

2 Large Dill Pickles
4 Hot Dog Rolls

4 Slices American
Cheese

1. Cut the dill pickles in fourths lengthwise.
2. Wrap two pickle slices in a cheese slice and put them inside the hot dog rolls.
3. Broil for a few minutes until cheese is melted and bubbly.

BAKED BEAN SANDWICH
Serves 2 or 3

2 Corn Muffins
1 Small Can Baked
Beans

4 Slices American
Cheese
4 Slices Bacon, cut in
half

1. Split the corn muffins and spread the baked beans on each half.
2. A slice of cheese goes on top, and then a criss-cross of two bacon halves.
3. Broil until cheese melts and bacon is crisp.

PINEAPPLE SALAD SANDWICH
Serves 2

4 Slices Canned
  Pineapple
Cottage Cheese

2 Maraschino Cherries
Lettuce Leaves

1. Place lettuce leaves on each salad plate and then one slice of pineapple.
2. Spread a thick layer of cottage cheese on the pineapple and add another slice of pineapple.
3. Top with cherries.

RED ROBIN
Serves 2 or 3

1 Can Tomato Soup
  (undiluted)
1 Cup American Cheese,
  grated

1 Egg, beaten
Salt & Pepper, dash
4 Slices Hot Toast

1. In top of a double boiler, mix the soup and cheese and cook slowly until cheese melts.
2. Add the beaten egg, salt and pepper.
3. Serve over hot toast.

Dinner

MIDGET MEAT LOAVES
Serves 4

½ Pound Ground Beef
2 Tablespoons Onion,
   minced

½ cup Bread Crumbs
1 Egg, beaten
Salt & Pepper, dash

1. Mix all ingredients together in a bowl.
2. Lightly grease cups in a muffin tin and fill with meat mixture.
3. Bake 15 minutes at 450 degrees.

When the loaves are done, they can be lifted out of the cups easily.

TUNA NOODLE FAVORITE
Serves 4

Wide Noodles (8 ounce
   box)
1 Can Tuna Fish
1 cup Cold Milk

1 can Cream of
   Mushroom Soup
   (undiluted)
1 cup Potato Chips,
   crushed

1. Cook noodles according to directions on the package.
2. Grease an 8 x 12 x 2-inch baking dish, and arrange noodles on bottom and tuna on top.
3. Mix the soup and milk in a bowl and pour over the noodles and tuna.
4. Sprinkle crushed potato chips over the top and bake in a 375 degree oven for 25 or 30 minutes until nicely browned.

EASY SPAGHETTI
Serves 3 or 4

½ Pound Ground Beef	½ teaspoon Salt
1 Onion, chopped	15½ ounce Can Spa-
1 Tablespoon Salad Oil	ghetti in Tomato Sauce

1. In a frying pan heat the oil and cook the onion until tender but not browned.
2. Add meat and cook, stirring, until brown.
3. Add the salt and can of spaghetti.
4. Cook until heated through.

TUTTI FRUITY PORK CHOPS
Serves 4

4 Pork Chops (thick)	1 Small Can Crushed
Garlic Salt	Pineapple
Pepper	1 cup Orange Juice

2 Tablespoons Salad Oil

1. Prepare the pork chops: Sprinkle with garlic salt and pepper. Heat oil in frying pan and brown chops 5 minutes on each side.
2. Arrange pork chops in a shallow baking dish.
3. Top each with a thick layer of crushed pineapple. Pour orange juice over chops.
4. Bake for one hour in a 350 degree oven.

BOSTON BAKED BEANS
AND FRANKS

Serves 4

4 Frankfurters	*1 teaspoon Dry Mustard*
1 Can Baked Beans	*1 Tablespoon Brown*
(medium size)	*Sugar*
2 Tablespoons Catsup	*2 Slices Bacon*

1. Slice the frankfurters in thirds lengthwise.
2. In a 1½ quart casserole dish, make layers:
   ⅓ can of beans
   frankfurter slices (use half)
   ⅓ can of beans
   dry mustard and catsup
   frankfurter slices (use other half)
   ⅓ can of beans
3. Sprinkle with brown sugar and crisscross the bacon slices on top.
4. Cover and bake for 30 minutes at 350 degrees.

HAWAIIAN THINGA KABOBS
Serves 4

1 Can Chopped Ham	1 Green Pepper
1 Can Pineapple Chunks	4 Skewers

1. Arrange your kabobs: Cut chopped ham into 1-inch cubes. Drain Pineapple chunks. Wash green pepper and cut into 1-inch squares.
2. Thread the skewers with green pepper, ham, pineapple, green pepper, ham, pineapple, making as many rows as you like.
3. Broil for several minutes until nicely browned.

Serve on skewers, or remove to a dinner plate.

PORCUPINES

Serves 4

1½ Pounds Ground
  Beef

½ cup Rice (regular
  rice, not instant,
  uncooked)

2 Tablespoons Onion,
  minced

1 teaspoon Salt

Pepper, dash

1 Can Tomato Soup
  (undiluted)

1 Soup Can Water

1. In a large bowl mix everything but soup and water together with a fork. Shape into large meatballs.

2. Mix the soup and water in a large frying pan and heat just to the boiling point, but don't boil.

3. Lower the heat and spoon the meatballs into the sauce.

4. Cook over low heat for one hour.

LEPRECHAUN PIE

Serves 4

16 ounce Can Beef Stew

1 Can Mushrooms

1 Package Refrigerated
  Biscuits

1. Mix the beef stew and mushrooms together in a casserole dish.

2. Place the biscuits on top so their sides touch.

3. Bake in a 350 degree oven for about 20 minutes until the biscuits are nicely browned.

INDIAN DINNER
Serves 4

1 Package Frozen Succotash, cooked
1 Can Tomato Sauce
12 Pork Sausages

1. Mix the succotash and tomato sauce in a baking dish.
2. Top with the pork sausages.
3. Bake at 350 degrees for about 20 minutes until sausages are browned.

CHICKEN LICKIN' A LA KING
Serves 4

1 Can Boned Chicken (or 2 cups left-over Chicken cut into bite size pieces)

1 Can Cream of Mushroom Soup (undiluted)

2 Pimentos, finely sliced

1 Small Can Peas (drained)

Salt and Pepper, dash

6 Patty Shells (baked)

1. In a saucepan mix everything except patty shells, and heat until steaming.
2. Serve over patty shells.

QUICK 'N EASY PIZZA
Serves 4

4 English Muffins   *1 Can Spaghetti Sauce*
Mozzarella Cheese, sliced   *with Meat*

1. Separate and toast the English muffins.
2. Spread the spaghetti sauce on the muffins and top with slices of cheese.
3. Broil for a few minutes until cheese melts and is gooey.

PANDORA'S SURPRISE SALAD
Serves 4

1 cup Cooked Ham   1 Green Pepper
1 cup Cheddar Cheese   1 Small Onion
1½ cups Lettuce Chunks   12 Cherry Tomatoes
Russian or French Dressing

1. Cut the ham and cheese in cubes and thinly slice the green pepper and onion.
2. Toss everything together in a salad bowl.
3. Pour on the dressing and toss again to mix dressing into the salad.

JACK-AND-THE-BEAN SALAD
Serves 4

1 Can String Beans   1 Tablespoon Sugar
2 Tablespoons Onion,   2 Tablespoons Salad Oil
  minced   2 Tablespoons Vinegar
½ teaspoon Salt   Lettuce Leaves
Pepper, dash

1. Drain juice from the can of string beans into a saucepan and add salt, pepper and sugar. Heat, stirring, until the liquid is hot, but do not boil.
2. In a large salad bowl mix salad oil, vinegar, string beans and minced onion.
3. Pour the liquid over the salad and toss lightly.
4. Chill for at least 30 minutes and serve on lettuce leaves.

FUNNY BUNNY SALAD
Serves 4

4 Canned Pear Halves   *4 Large Marshmallows*

Whole Cloves   *Lettuce Leaves*

2 Bananas

1. Arrange lettuce leaves on salad plates.

2. Place pear halves on lettuce, flat side down.

3. Slice bananas lengthwise and then crosswise, and place them at small end of pear for the bunnies' ears.

4. Make the eyes and mouths with the cloves and the tails with the marshmallows.

BALONEY BLOSSOMS
Serves 4

1 Package Instant Mashed Potatoes

4 Slices Bologna   *1 Green Pepper*

1. Cook enough instant mashed potatoes for 4. (Follow directions on package.) Spoon out into flat dishes.

2. Gently fold bologna slices in half and cut out tulip or any flower shape. Place this on top of the potato.

3. Cut pieces of green pepper for stems and leaves. Place these on the potato.

Desserts

ICE CREAM SNOWBALLS
Serves 4

1 Pint Ice Cream (any flavor)   *Cherries*
½ cup Shredded Coconut   *Chocolate Sauce*

1. Pour shredded coconut into a small bowl.
2. With an ice cream scoop, dip out balls of ice cream and drop, one at a time, into the coconut. Roll around to coat evenly.
3. Serve in dessert dishes and dribble chocolate sauce over the top. Dot with a cherry.

JUNIOR BANANA SPLITS
Serves 4

4 Bananas   *Jar Pineapple Topping*
1 Pint Ice Cream   *Canned Whipped*
Maraschino Cherries   *Topping*

1. Peel the bananas and slice them lengthwise and then crosswise.
2. In flat dessert dishes arrange the bananas in a 4-pointed cross, rounded ends out.
3. Put a scoop of ice cream on top of the bananas.
4. Spoon on the pineapple topping, some whipped cream topping, and dot with a cherry.

PEACH SUNDAE
Serves 4

4 Peach Halves (canned or fresh)
1 Pint Vanilla Ice Cream
1 Package Frozen Raspberries (thawed)

1. Arrange peach halves in dessert dishes.
2. Spoon ice cream into peaches.
3. Top with raspberries.

CHOCOLATE MARSHMALLOW SMUDGE
Serves 4

1 Pint Chocolate Ice Cream
1 Jar Marshmallow Topping
Fudge Sauce

1. Scoop out ice cream into four dessert dishes.
2. Spoon on marshmallow topping and dribble fudge sauce over the top.

ORANGE-ON-ORANGE GELATIN
Serves 4

1 Package Orange Gelatin

11 ounce Can Mandarin Oranges (save juice in measuring cup)

1 cup Boiling Water

1. Mix gelatin with boiling water and stir until dissolved.
2. Drain liquid from oranges into a measuring cup and add enough cold water to make 1 cup. Stir into gelatin.
3. Divide the orange slices among four dessert dishes and pour gelatin over them.
4. Place in the refrigerator until the gelatin is set.

LIMEY FLUFF
Serves 4

1 Package Lime Gelatin

Miniature Marshmallows

1. Make a layer of miniature marshmallows in the cups of a muffin tin.
2. Prepare gelatin as package directs.
3. Pour over marshmallows and refrigerate until gelatin is set.
4. Run warm water over bottom of muffin tin for just a minute when ready to serve. Limey Fluffs will fall out easily.

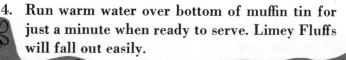

BAKED APPLES
Serves 4

4 Large Red Cooking Apples   *2 Tablespoons*
¾ cup Granulated Sugar   *Brown Sugar*
1 cup Water

1. Prepare apples: Wash and core. Peel ⅓ of the way down from the top. Place stem end down in a baking dish.

2. Boil the granulated sugar and water for 10 minutes. Pour over the apples.

3. Bake in a 350 degree oven about 45 minutes until apples are tender when pierced with a fork.

4. Remove from the oven and sprinkle on brown sugar. Return to oven until sugar is melted.

FLUFFY ORANGE MALLOW
Serves 4

¼ pound Marshmallows   *¾ cup Orange Juice*
½ cup Heavy Cream

1. Place the marshmallows and orange juice in a saucepan over low heat and stir until the marshmallows melt.

2. Set in the refrigerator until mixture thickens slightly.

3. Whip the cream and gently stir into the orange mixture.

4. Pour into sherbet glasses and refrigerate for several hours before serving.

HIDE-AND-SEEK PUDDING
Serves 4

1 Package Vanilla Instant Pudding
4 Teaspoons Jam or Jelly

1. Make the pudding according to the package directions.
2. Pour into dessert dishes and place in the refrigerator to set.
3. When the pudding is set use a teaspoon to scoop out a spoonful of pudding, leaving the pudding on the spoon. Fill the hole with some jam or jelly and replace the spoonful of pudding on top.

Surprise, when you dig in!

MONKEY'S DELIGHT
Serves 4

Sunday Morning Breakfast Salad (page 14)
1 cup Heavy Cream   1 teaspoon Vanilla
3 Tablespoons Sugar

1. Make the Sunday Morning Breakfast Salad and refrigerate.
2. In a chilled bowl, start beating the cream and when slightly thick, but still soupy, stir in vanilla and sugar.
3. Continue beating until cream is whipped and a little stiff.
4. When ready to serve the fruit, pour on whipped cream and toss until fruit is coated. Serve in any kind of dessert dish.

APPLE SAUCE AND ICE CREAM
Serves 2 or 3

1 Medium Can or Jar Apple Sauce
½ teaspoon Cinnamon   Vanilla Ice Cream

1. In a saucepan warm the apple sauce and stir in the cinnamon.
2. Spoon out into dessert dishes and top with a scoop of ice cream. Serve immediately.

CHERRY SMASH DESSERT
Serves 4

1 Package Cherry Gelatin
1 cup Hot Water
1 Pint Cherry-Vanilla Ice Cream
½ teaspoon Lemon Juice
1 Medium Can Sweet Cherries (drained)

1. Mix the gelatin with hot water. Stir until it is dissolved.
2. Add ice cream and stir until melted. Stir in lemon juice.
3. Mash cherries with a fork and pour into the gelatin. Stir the mixture well.
4. Place in the refrigerator to set and spoon out into dessert dishes to serve.

Beverages

ORANGE EGGNOG
Serves 2

1 cup Cold Milk   *¼ teaspoon vanilla*
1 Raw Egg   *¼ cup Orange Juice*
            1 Tablespoon Powdered Sugar

1. Mix everything together in a bowl and beat for two minutes with an egg beater.
2. Pour into glasses and share with a friend.

BLACK COW
Serves 2

Vanilla Ice Cream   *Root Beer, ice cold*

1. Put two scoops of vanilla ice cream in two tall glasses.
2. Slowly fill the glass with root beer.

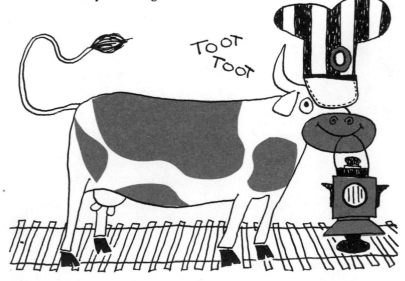

PEACH FUZZ
Serves 2

1 cup Cold Water
*3 Tablespoons Strained
Peaches (Baby Food)*

1 Tablespoon Honey
¼ cup Nonfat Dry Milk

1. In a shaker or large glass jar with a top, mix and stir the water, peaches and honey.
2. Sprinkle in the dry milk and shake well.
3. Pour into a very tall glass for one large serving, or divide in half for two.

FROSTED STRAWBERRY FLOAT
Serves 4

½ Pint Box Strawberries
¼ cup Sugar
3 cups Milk (cold)

*½ Pint Strawberry
Ice Cream*

1. Prepare berries: Wash, drain and remove stems. Mash with a fork in a small bowl.
2. Stir in sugar and milk gradually, beating with an egg beater.
3. Add ice cream and stir until it starts to melt.

Serve in tall glasses.

CHOCOLATE MINT SHAKE
1 Serving

2 Tablespoons Chocolate Syrup

1 cup Milk (cold)

1 Large Scoop Peppermint Ice Cream

1. Mix everything together in a bowl and beat with an egg beater.
2. Serve in a tall glass.

GRAPE-ALE COOLER
1 Serving

½ cup Grape Juice   *Crushed Ice*

½ cup Ginger Ale (cold)   *Ice Cream*

1. In a tall glass mix the grape juice and ginger ale.
2. Add the crushed ice and a scoop of ice cream.

PINK ELEPHANTS
For a Party, 6 to 8 Servings

1 can Frozen Lemonade   Maraschino Cherries
2 cups Cranberry Juice

1. In a large pitcher mix the lemonade as the label on the can directs.
2. Add the cranberry juice and stir.
3. Pour over ice cubes and serve a straw in each glass with a cherry on top.

BANANA SMOOTHIE SHAKE
1 Serving

1 Ripe Banana   ½ teaspoon Vanilla
1 cup Milk (cold)   1 Scoop Vanilla Ice Cream

1. Peel the banana and mash with a fork in a bowl.
2. Add the milk and vanilla and beat until well mixed.
3. Pour into a tall glass and float a scoop of ice cream on top.

LEMON-ORANGE COOLER
Serves 4

⅓ cup Frozen Orange
   Juice Concentrate

3 Tablespoons Honey

¾ cup Crushed Ice

2 cups Milk

1 Pint Lemon Sherbet

1. Stir orange juice concentrate and honey in a 1 quart jar with a top.
2. Add ice and milk and shake.
3. Put scoops of sherbet in 4 tall glasses and pour orange mixture over the top.

FRUIT FROSTIES
1 Serving

Frozen Juice Concentrate (orange, grape or your favorite flavor)
1 cup Crushed Ice

1. Fill a paper cup with crushed ice.
2. Pour several Tablespoonfuls of the juice concentrate over the ice and sip slowly.

DOUBLE STRAWBERRY SODA
1 Serving

Strawberry Ice Cream   *Ginger Ale*
Strawberry Jam

1. Put two scoops of strawberry ice cream in a large glass.
2. Top with a Tablespoonful of strawberry jam.
3. Fill with ginger ale.

PEACHES 'N CREAM FLOAT
1 Serving

Peach Ice Cream   *Cream Soda*

1. Put a scoop of peach ice cream in a large glass and fill with cream soda.

MOBY DICK
1 Serving

Vanilla Ice Cream   *Grape Soda*

1. Put a scoop of vanilla ice cream in a large glass and fill with grape soda.

OCEAN BREEZE
1 Serving

Lime Sherbet   *Lemon Soda*

1. Put a scoop of lime sherbet in a large glass and fill with lemon soda.

Nibblers & TV Snacks

POPCORN

½ cup Hard Yellow   2 Tablespoons Cooking Oil
  Corn for Popping   ½ Stick Butter, melted

1. Heat the oil in a heavy pan with a lid.
2. When the oil looks hot or "wavy," pour in the corn and quickly place the lid on the pot.
3. Carefully shake the pan over medium heat until all the popping stops.
4. Put the popcorn in a large bowl and pour melted butter over the top. Sprinkle with salt and mix well.

PEANUT BUTTER CANDY

⅓ cup Peanut Butter   32 Marshmallows
¼ cup Butter (½ Stick)   Vegetable Shortening
5 cups Crunchy Cereal

1. Grease a mixing bowl with shortening. Place cereal in the bowl.
2. In a double boiler melt marshmallows, peanut butter and butter.
3. Pour over the cereal and stir until all the cereal is coated.
4. Pack the candy mixture into a greased cake pan and cool. Cut into squares.

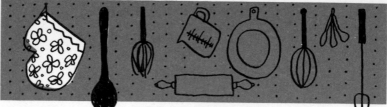

BROWNIES

1 cup Sifted Flour	½ cup Butter or Vegetable Shortening
1 Egg	
1 cup Chocolate Syrup	½ teaspoon Salt
½ cup Sugar	½ cup Chopped Nuts

1. Mix the egg, chocolate sauce and butter in a bowl. Mix well for at least 2 minutes.
2. In another bowl sift flour, sugar and salt. Stir the dry mixture into the wet mixture and add nuts.
3. Grease an 8- or 9-inch square cake pan and pour the brownie batter in the pan.
4. Bake for 30 minutes at 350 degrees. Cool and cut into squares.

CHOCOLATE KISSES

3 Egg Whites	2 ounces unsweetened Baking Chocolate, grated
½ cup Sugar	
	½ teaspoon Vanilla

1. Beat the egg whites until they are stiff.
2. Add sugar, chocolate and vanilla.
3. Grease a cookie sheet and sprinkle lightly with flour.
4. Drop kisses by teaspoonfuls on cookie sheet and bake at 250 degrees for about 45 minutes.

CARAMEL APPLES

6 or 7 Small Apples　　　　*2 Tablespoons*
Wooden Sticks for each apple　*Cold Water*
14 ounce Package Caramels

1.　Wash and dry the apples and put a stick into the stem end of each.

2.　In a saucepan over low heat melt the caramels and water. Stir until caramels are a smooth sauce.

3.　Holding the apples by the sticks, dip them into the caramel sauce, turning them around to coat evenly. Scrape the bottom of the apples with a knife to remove excess caramel.

4.　Place the apples on a greased cookie sheet and chill in the refrigerator until caramel is firm and apples are chilled.

FIVE-MINUTE FUDGE

6 ounce Can Evaporated Milk
1⅔ cups Sugar
½ teaspoon Salt
½ cup Chopped Walnuts

1½ cups Miniature
  Marshmallows
1½ cups Semi-Sweet
  Chocolate Bits

1 teaspoon Vanilla

1. In a medium saucepan mix evaporated milk, sugar and salt. Heat to the boiling point, but do not boil. Reduce heat and simmer for 5 minutes.

2. Remove from heat and add walnuts, marshmallows, chocolate bits and vanilla. Stir until smooth.

3. Pour into a greased 9-inch square cake pan. Cool and cut into squares.

PEANUT BRITTLE

1 cup Water
2 cups Sugar
*½ cup Light Corn
  Syrup*

2 cups Unsalted Peanuts
1 teaspoon Butter
*¼ teaspoon Baking
  Soda*

1. In a medium saucepan mix sugar, corn syrup and water. Stir over low heat about 15 minutes, or until the mixture reaches 238 degrees on a candy thermometer.
2. Add peanuts and cook until the syrup turns golden (about 10 minutes). Add butter and baking soda, stirring only until they are well mixed.
3. Pour onto a greased cookie sheet, forming a large square of brittle. Cool and break into pieces.

COCONUT TREATS

2 tablespoons Butter
¼ cup Brown Sugar

*2 Tablespoons Flaked
  Coconut*

6 Graham Crackers

1. Blend the sugar into the butter with a fork or spoon. Mix in the coconut.
2. Spread on graham crackers.
3. Toast in the broiler on a sheet of aluminum foil wrapped around a cookie sheet.

CHOCOLATE ANIMAL CRACKERS

1 Box Animal Crackers

1 Package Semi-Sweet Chocolate Bits

*1 Tablespoon Vegetable Shortening (do not use
butter or margerine)*

1. Melt chocolate bits and shortening in a sauce-
    pan over low heat. Stir until smooth.
2. Dip animal crackers into chocolate and lift out
    with a fork.
3. Place on waxed paper to harden.

TOPSY TURVY

1 Bag Popcorn (already popped)
1 Can Peanuts (salted)
1 Medium Box Raisins

1. In a large serving bowl mix everything together.

This is a good party snack.

SHAGGY DOGS

1 Can Sweet Condensed Milk
5 or 6 Slices White Bread
¾ cup Shredded Coconut

1. Trim crusts off the bread and cut into 1-inch squares.
2. Pour condensed milk in one bowl and coconut in another. Dip the bread squares first in the milk and then in the coconut.
3. Place on a cookie sheet and broil 4 inches from the heat. Watch carefully so they don't burn. When golden brown remove to a platter to cool.

Holidays and Special Occasions
Birthdays

ICE CREAM CLOWNS FOR A PARTY
Serves 4. Double the recipe if you're having a party!

1 Pint Vanilla Ice Cream   *12 Raisins*
4 Sugar Cones   *8 Chocolate Bits*
4 Maraschino Cherries   *Whipped Cream*

1. Place scoops (balls) of ice cream on dessert plates.
2. Top each ice cream ball with a sugar cone for the clown's hat; place two chocolate bits for eyes, three raisins for the mouth and a cherry for the nose.
3. Put whipped cream around the clown for his neck ruffle.

BIRTHDAY CANDLE SALAD
Serves 4

4 Slices Pineapple   *2 Bananas*
4 Lettuce Leaves   *4 Cherries*

1. On lettuce leaves on salad plates arrange the pineapple slices.
2. Peel the bananas and slice in half crosswise. Stand the bananas in the pineapple holes, rounded end up.
3. Press a cherry on top of the banana for the candle flame.

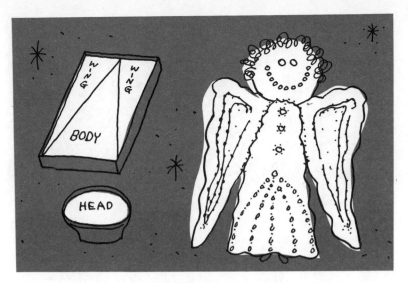

CHRISTMAS ANGEL

1 Box Cake Mix (White or Yellow)
1 Can White Refrigerated Frosting
Decorating Sugars, Silver Dragées, Little Candies

1. Mix the cake batter according to the package instructions and bake in an oblong pan (12 x 8 inches). Save a little batter and make one cupcake (for the angel's head).

2. When the cake is baked and cool, cut into sections as the picture shows: one large triangle for the angel's body, and two triangles for the wings.

3. Arrange the cake sections on a large platter, as the picture shows, for the body, wings and head.

4. Frost the sides and top of the cake and decorate with the little candies, dragées and decorating sugars.

53

EGGNOG
Serves 4-6

4 Eggs	*1 teaspoon Vanilla*
4 Tablespoons Sugar	*4 cups Milk*
¼ teaspoon Salt	*Nutmeg*

1. With an egg beater mix the eggs, sugar and salt and beat until thick and lemon-colored.
2. Add vanilla and milk and beat until well mixed.
3. Pour into a punch bowl and sprinkle with nutmeg.

Serve in punch cups or small glasses.

Valentine's Day

VALENTINE HEART'S DELIGHT
Serves 4

1 Package Cherry Gelatin
1 Small Package Red Candy Hearts
Canned Whipped Cream

1. Prepare gelatin as the package directs. Pour into cups of a muffin tin and place in the refrigerator until the gelatin begins to thicken.
2. Drop a candy heart into each and return to the refrigerator to set.
3. When ready to serve, run a little warm water over the bottom of the muffin tin for just a few seconds. The tarts can then be easily removed.
4. Serve in dessert dishes and top with whipped cream and another candy heart on top.

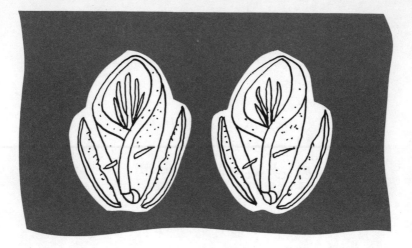

Easter

EASTER LILIES
Serves 4

3 Hard-Cooked Eggs
1 Tablespoon
  Mayonnaise
1 teaspoon Onion,
  (finely chopped)
¼ teaspoon Salt

Pepper, dash
1 teaspoon Vinegar
4 Long, Thin Carrot
  Sticks
8 Thin Dill Pickle Slices
  (Sliced Lengthwise)

1. Chop the eggs and add mayonnaise, onion, salt and pepper. Add vinegar and mash into a smooth paste.
2. Trim crusts off bread and spread egg paste on bread slices.
3. Fasten two opposite corners together with a toothpick (as picture shows).
4. Decorate with a carrot stick for the center of the lily and pickle slices for leaves.

COTTONTAIL PUFFS

1 Egg (separate yolk
    from white)

1/2 cup Butter or Margerine

1/4 cup Sugar

1 teaspoon Almond Extract

1 1/4 cups Sifted Flour

2 Tablespoons Milk

3/4 cup Nuts
    (finely chopped)

1. With electric mixer beat the butter, sugar, almond extract and egg yolk.
2. Gradually add the flour and milk, still beating the mixture, until it is a stiff dough.
3. With your hands make small balls of the dough and place on a cookie sheet.
4. Beat the egg white until stiff and brush a little on each puff. Then sprinkle with nuts and bake in a 400 degree oven for 12 minutes.

Mother's Day

What a nice surprise for mother to have her breakfast prepared for her by you and Dad. You could serve scrambled eggs and bacon and these extra special Mother's Day Doughnuts.

MOTHER'S DAY DOUGHNUTS
Serves 4

4 Sugared Doughnuts   Butter
Brown Sugar

1. Slice the doughnuts crosswise and place on a cookie sheet, sugar side down.
2. Butter the doughnuts and sprinkle with brown sugar.
3. Broil for a few minutes until sugar is melted and bubbly.

Father's Day

HAPPY FATHER'S DAY CAKE

1 Package Cake Mix (Dad's favorite kind)
1 Can White Refrigerated Frosting
Alphabet Cereal
1 Plain Chocolate Bar

1. Bake the cake according to instructions on the package. Frost with white icing. (You may need a little help from a grownup.)

2. Here's the trick to making the cake special for Dad. Select letters from the alphabet cereal for "HAPPY FATHER'S DAY" or any other words you would like to say.

3. Melt chocolate in a small saucepan over very low heat. Dip the letters in the chocolate and lift out with a fork. Place them right side up on waxed paper to dry.

4. Arrange "HAPPY FATHER'S DAY" words from chocolate letters and place the cake in front of Dad. Everyone can enjoy Dad's cake.

59

Fourth of July

JULY FOURTH PUDDING
Serves 6

1 Package Whipped Cream Dessert Topping Mix
½ cup Milk   ½ teaspoon Vanilla
¼ cup Sugar   Red and Blue Decorating Sugar
⅓ cup Shredded Coconut

1. Chill a bowl in the refrigerator before starting. Then beat the topping mix with milk. When stiff add sugar and vanilla. Beat until sugar is blended.

2. Place six cupcake paper cups in a muffin tin and spoon the pudding into them. Freeze in the freezing compartment of your refrigerator.

3. When ready to serve, remove paper cups and place the puddings on dessert plates, small end down.

4. Sprinkle red sugar on one side and blue on the other. Now sprinkle shredded coconut down the middle.

There you have it — patriotic pudding!

Halloween

CHEESE O'LANTERNS

1 pound American   *Green*
   Cheese (orange or   *Pepper*
   dark yellow colored)   *Slivers*

1. Cut cheese into chunks about 1½ inches.
2. Roll in the palms of your hands to make balls. Squash a little on top and bottom to make the balls pumpkin-shaped.
3. With the back of a knife make about six ridges in each pumpkin from top to bottom.
4. Stick green pepper slivers in the tops to make the pumpkin stem. Store in the refrigerator until ready to serve.

HALLOWEEN WITCHES' BREW

Orange Sherbet   *Ginger Ale*

1. Place a scoop of orange sherbet in a tall glass.
2. Pour ginger ale slowly over the sherbet.

Thanksgiving

NAME-TAG PIE

Pumpkin Pie (from Cream, (Several
* the bakery)   Tablespoons)*
*   3 ounce Package Cream Cheese*

1. Let the cream cheese stand at room temperature until it is soft. Add several Tablespoonfuls of cream to make it like soft icing.
2. Roll a sheet of paper into a cone shape and cut a tiny hole in the bottom.
3. Fill cone about ⅓ full of cream cheese mixture.
4. Gently squeeze the cone and write names on the pumpkin pie before serving at dinner.

CRANBERRY-APPLE SAUCE

1 cup Cranberries (raw) ½ cup Water
2 cups Chopped Apple ½ cup Sugar

1. Cook the fruit in water over low heat until soft.
2. Mash through a coarse strainer and add sugar. Stir until sugar is dissolved.
3. Chill before serving.

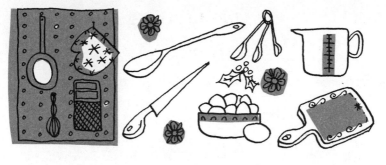

Glossary

Baking is cooking in the oven at a certain temperature. The recipe will tell you how hot the oven should be.

Beating of Egg Whites must be done with bowl and beater free from grease. Use a rotary beater or electric mixer and beat until stiff peaks form.

Boiling is cooking a liquid in a pot over high heat until bubbles rise and break on the surface.

Broiling is quick cooking at high heat, directly under the flame or heating coil in the oven.

Chop food by cutting into small pieces with a knife.

Dash is a very small amount — less than your smallest measuring spoon.

Grating is making little shreds by rubbing the food on a "grater."

Grease a pan by rubbing it with butter or vegetable shortening.

Mince food by chopping very fine.

Peeling is removing the skin from the fruit or vegetable.

Separate Eggs by gently cracking shells and holding yolk in one shell half while letting the white drip into a bowl; then drop the yolk in another bowl.

Simmering is boiling over very low heat so that little bubbles break around the edges of the pot.

Toss your salad by lifting gently with two forks or two spoons.

Whip Cream in a chilled bowl with chilled beaters. When cream is soupy, add vanilla and sugar. Beat again until cream is slightly stiff.